SINGLE BY CHOICE OR CHANCE

Single by Choice or Chance

The smart woman's guide to living longer, better

Jill O'Donnell & Jackie Porter

INSOMNIAC PRESS

Library and Archives Canada Cataloguing in Publication

O'Donnell, Jill, 1940-, author
Single by choice or chance / Jill O'Donnell & Jackie Porter.

Issued in print and electronic formats.
ISBN 978-1-55483-170-8 (paperback).--ISBN 978-1-55483-184-5
(html)

1. Single people--Canada--Finance, Personal. 2. Retirement--
Planning. 3. Single people--Life skills guides. I. Porter, Jackie, 1970-,
author II. Title.

| HG179.O366 2016 | 332.0240086'52 | C2016-902029-0 |
| | | C2016-902030-4 |

Printed and bound in Canada

Insomniac Press
520 Princess Avenue, London, Ontario, Canada, N6B 2B8
www.insomniacpress.com

Contents

CHAPTER 1

Love Your Life
Before You Leave It

*And in the end, it's not the years in your life that
count. It's the life in your years.*
— Edward J. Stieglitz

You're single, aging and thinking about the future. You continue to save for a rainy day. In doing so, you also need to consider who you are and what you will do for the rest of your life.

Forget retirement. Think end of working, and then it's up to you to decide when that will be. Things to think about include:

- **Where to live?**
- **What to do?**
- **Caring for an aging parent**
- **Caring for yourself**
- **How much will it all cost?**

Facts

- The average age of a widow in Canada is 56
- Since 2015, there are more people over the age of 65 than under 15
- The fastest growing segment of the population is the over-85 age group
- Women outlive men by three years

The goal of this book is to help single women find the best ways to live a long, healthy financial life.

Women are single by choice or chance. Not every woman has a partner; some choose to remain single. About 5% of single women over 65 years of age have never married.

Over the past 50 years, women's roles have significantly changed from the proverbial housewife to career women of today. Still, many women earn less than men despite great strides in education and career placement. Others have fewer years' pension contribution because of career interruptions (raising children), contract positions or no pension plan available to them.

Single by choice

- preferred lifestyle
- could be single with or without children
- 5% of women over 65 have never married

Single by chance

- chosen singlehood after unsatisfactory relationships
- never found the right partner
- widowed (with or without pension)
- divorced

We know that women earn less than men; women take on contract positions with fewer resources; and fewer women have pensions.

Statistics to consider
- 43% of Canadian women over 65 are single
- 8% are separated or divorced
- 30% are widowed

Women previously relegated to the service professions such as nursing, teaching and physical and occupational therapies changed the landscape when they began enrolling in medicine, law, engineering, architecture and business, opening doors for them to move into the corporate world. Women are now entrepreneurs and chief executive officers of major corporations. Many become active board members making a difference in the way business is done.

When separation occurs in mid-life, women without a specific profession or trade will not have good work opportunities open to them. Those with qualifications who have not worked for many years will need to upgrade them, but they may not have the resources to return to school, may therefore end up in lower paying positions.

If you have paid into the Canada Pension Plan but took time off to have children, you may be eligible for shared benefits from your spouse. Discussion with your lawyer and financial planner will reveal what you are entitled to.

Nobody is ever prepared for widowhood. Life changes when you lose a spouse. There are so many things to think about: arranging the funeral, applying for benefits, where you will live, putting your finances in order and coping with your loss emotionally, to name just a few. The Service Canada website explains what a survivor is entitled to upon the death of her spouse: www.servicecanada.gc.ca.

We've put together composites of five ladies—Charlotte, Beth, Olga, Samantha and Karima. Perhaps you will find aspects of their lives that match your situation.

Charlotte

Charlotte spent her working life as a television producer. She loved her career, but the jobs were always on a contract basis. Fortunately, for the last ten years, Charlotte was employed full-time. She lives in a well-appointed one-bedroom rental apartment filled with artefacts collected on her many trips around the world. It is close to shops, amenities and entertainment in the heart of her city. Instead of investing in real estate, Charlotte chose to invest in a collection of Canadian art. In 2008, when the financial crisis hit everyone, she lost a large portion of her financial portfolio and at that point decided to work until she was 70 to make up for her losses because she had only a small pension.

Over the years, Charlotte had an on-again, off-again relationship with a gentleman friend, however they always maintained separate residences. Since his death a few years ago, she has chosen to just enjoy life as a single woman.

Charlotte lived life to the fullest and was delighted when she was transferred on business to New York City for a couple of years in the '80s. She took in all the culture that city had to offer: Broadway shows, the Lincoln Center, jazz, Central Park events and the plethora of art galleries. Her travels have taken her to the ends of the earth, and she is a wonderful storyteller about those trips.

A lover of good food and wine, Charlotte enjoys entertaining both at home and in fine restaurants. She is happy living in the city because it is filled with art and culture.

Her only living relative, a nephew, lives in another city. Although they maintain contact, they are not close. She has no children. Luckily, she does have a few very close friends who are always there for her.

Shortly after her 68th birthday, Charlotte was given an early buyout package. Totally unprepared for retirement, it hit her very hard, as she had hoped to work until she turned 70. She was stuck on stop, unable to make any major decisions, and ended up in hospital. She was affected even more when she developed cardiac symptoms and needed stent implants. Now 71, after many hospitalizations and therapy, she has begun to focus on her future by getting involved in meaningful volunteerism. Leaving work left a huge void in her life.

Olga

Olga, aged 55, should be in the prime of her life. She has been a stay-at-home parent, fantastic home cook (her borscht is second to none) and, in the old-fashioned vernacular, a "housewife" or "homemaker" since her marriage to Alexei 32 years ago. The physical demands of raising youngsters are in the distant past, as her children, Lina and Dimitri, are 30 and 27 years old, respectively. Alexei was a tool and die maker, and Olga never worked for pay (but worked very, very hard for her family), so they learned from a young age to be frugal and watch their pennies. However, children are expensive, and both Olga and Alexei found it difficult to deny Lina and Dimitri anything they wanted. At times, they dipped into their retirement savings to ensure that their children did not "suffer." Olga and Alexei had moved to Canada when Olga was 24 to give their children a better life, and they were willing to sacrifice a luxurious retirement to give their children a leg up. Olga and Alexei figured that their OAS and Alexei's CPP would be enough money in retirement, when added to the small amount of savings that they had not yet spent on the children.

Olga's dreams of growing old with Alexei were shattered when she tragically lost her husband to a heart attack at age 58. She is currently still living in the family home with Lina and Dimitri, who are unmarried with no children of their own. Lina and Dimitri have no plans to move out anytime soon, especially now that they have lost their father, and they feel that their mother needs them more than ever. Lina and Dimitri are only sporadically employed, and would have a hard time covering their living expenses if they resided elsewhere. In fact, Olga cooks for them every day and often does their laundry.

Alexei used to do all the banking and gave Olga a weekly allowance for groceries and other household items. Olga knows that there must be bills to pay for utilities, property taxes and mortgage payments, but she does not know how much is owing or whether she will have any money left to live on after she pays the bills. As far as she knows, Alexei did not have life insurance, and she is sick with worry about how she and the children will survive.

Beth

At 58, Beth did not expect she and John would ever separate. It was very difficult for her, as her parents emigrated from Korea and feel strongly that marriage is a sacred bond, not to be cast aside lightly. For this and other reasons, Beth waited for their daughter Mary to become financially self-sufficient before she left John. Mary, now 27, lives in a rented condo. She is a first-year associate with a large law firm.

Having been a legal secretary for the past 31 years, Beth plans to work until she is 67. She enjoys her job, makes a decent income, has a sizeable locked-in retirement savings plan from a previous employer and also has an unlocked retirement savings plan with her current employer.

Beth, the financier of the family, knew to the penny their assets and liabilities. Her family lawyer was thrilled she had this knowledge, and it proved to be extremely helpful when calculating the equalization payment she would receive from John as a result of their separation. Beth looked after all monetary matters, creating the family's budget and ensuring everyone stuck to the plan. Before the separation, it was not overly challenging to adhere to the budget, as there were two incomes and only one household to maintain. Now, with just one income, Beth must worry about managing her own financial needs.

John was allowed to keep the family home. Beth received a sufficient payment from John that gave her a generous nest egg. Currently, she is renting an apartment near work while researching various neighbourhoods before buying any real estate.

Recently, Beth was diagnosed with slowly progressive multiple sclerosis and would prefer to live in a condo until she requires an assisted living facility, many years from now, she hopes. Now separated for six months, she is anxious to get on with her divorce.

Beth is confident her financial resources will support her for the rest of her life. She is careful with her money, has enough to have fun and travel if she so chooses and has purchased long-term care insurance, as she cannot rely on Mary to care for her in her elder years.

As often happens in a separation, Beth has lost some long-term friends. She is now eager to meet new ones but is unsure how to begin.

Wanting to follow her parents' lead in financially taking care of her children, Beth would like to be able to give Mary financial help if she needs it, just like her parents did for her in the past and now again since her separation. Beth, an only child, knows she will receive a generous inheritance from them.

Having sacrificed her own happiness for the past 27 years for the sake of her family, Beth is keen to move on to a future filled with purpose and happiness.

Samantha

This is not what Samantha thought her life would look like after being married for 20 years. Samantha is a 47-year-old nurse looking for work. Growing up in Barbados, she took her basic nurse training in the United Kingdom. That is where she met Barry, a Canadian studying abroad. He brought her to Canada where they were married. Shortly after they were married, Samantha sponsored her parents to move to Canada. She immediately enrolled at university to do her degree in nursing. Unfortunately, she quit when she became pregnant.

After raising Jessica, now 16, and Sam, aged 12, and devoting her life to her marriage, Samantha divorced Barry. Despite taking Barry to court on many occasions to have him pay child support, it never happened. She eventually gave up. It was then Samantha thought it would be easier to move in with her parents and finish her nursing degree that was put on hold after she got married. It took her almost two years to update her credits and finish. Samantha is grateful for the support she has from her parents. She can't imagine what her life would have been like without them.

Recently, a nursing agency offered Samantha a contract supervisory position close to home. It couldn't have come at a better time. Right now, Samantha needs to get back on her feet financially, as she is about to use up what is left of her savings.

It has been a hard road over the past few years. Scraping by to pay the bills without help meant she had to cash in just about everything she owned. She had no idea how much debt she and Barry had until it was too late. She had left it up to Barry to take care of the finances.

Unfortunately, Barry started to have problems with depression and alcoholism in the last five years of their marriage. One day he came home and something was different. He just checked out of his life. He withdrew from Samantha, the kids and his work. Often he would have violent outbursts or disappear for a few days at a time. He stopped paying the bills. It was a very stressful and frightening time for Samantha, who had been a stay-at-home mom since the kids were born. That was the traditional life she and Barry had always wanted.

CHAPTER 2

Designing Your Own Future

The journey of a thousand miles begins with a single step.
—Lao Tzu

How do you perceive your future? Making plans now will mean an easier transition to when you are no longer working. The best way to manage that is to create a **life plan**, a map as to how you will achieve that end. A life plan is very personal, focusing on non-financial goals such as health, personal fulfillment and family involvement without losing sight of the need to save and invest for the future. Your financial planner can guide you through the maze of options and help you select those that best suit your needs. First, you need to define your vision and set some personal goals, develop a strategic plan and then an action plan to help put you where you want to be tomorrow.

Define your vision for the rest of your life and set some personal goals.

Develop a strategic life plan.

Determine who you are: look into the future to assemble a picture of where you want to be.

Now that **Beth** has separated, she definitely needs to put a life plan in place. As a single person who has to rely on a single income, she needs to be diligent about setting realistic goals. She still has another nine or ten years to work, so this is the best time to map out her future. Beth needs to set short-, medium- and long-term goals and then make sure they are achievable.

Let your vision become your compass as you chart your life's journey

Would you plan a trip around the world without considering how you are going to get there, where you want to go, when you are going to do it and why it is important to you? Of course not! That is why you need to focus on a life plan.

The future belongs to those who believe in the power of their dreams

Hard hit by her divorce, **Samantha** has a difficult road ahead of her. However difficult it may be, she still needs to think about the future and work through where she wants to be when she is no longer working. Luckily, she now has a contract nursing position. That is a start. Now she needs to develop a **mission statement**.

Creating a Mission Statement

- Keep a journal and make frequent entries.
- What in the past has made you feel safe and secure or the most challenged?
- When did you feel most loved and valued?
- Where were you most able to use your abilities or talents or pursue your greatest interests in a

satisfying way?
- Reflect on the past with a view to the future.
- Think about people, places and events—there may be clues to who you are and what matters to you.

First, Samantha needs to set **realistic goals**. Here are some suggestions for her:
1. I want to start paying down my debts.
2. I want to work towards having my own living space.
3. I want to ensure my children's education is completed.

Samantha's **mission statement** might be: To focus my life on getting out of debt, securing a place of my own where we can live and grow as a family and ensure my children receive their proper education. Setting her **action plan** will be her next step. Meeting with her financial planner will help her focus on putting her life together.

Dreams do come true. Putting a plan together means realizing those dreams. Describe what you want to achieve, rather than how you will do it. Try to describe specific ends without being too specific about how they might be achieved.

Karima has charted her life plan without really writing it down. Her goal of paying off her house as quickly as possible will soon be realized. Saving for her retirement has always been paramount. Her desire to find a life partner may or may not materialize, so she still needs to address her future hopes and dreams. She now needs to work on her estate planning, getting her powers of attorney and will in order. It will mean doing some-soul searching as to whom she chooses for the roles of powers of attorney for personal care and property, perhaps sitting down with one of her closest friends to see if they would be willing to take on such a role and then making sure it is put into place.

Set goals: make lists
Short term: within the next two years
Intermediate term: within two to ten years
Long term: beyond ten years

Consider personal relationships, health, family, education and career, community, leisure time and finances.

Research to make sure you have up-to-date information about what you want to achieve.

Analyze your situation.

Are there special requirements such as financial or educational requirements you need to meet first?

Are your goals realistic?

Do you have the time, money and skills required? If not, how can you change your goals to make them more achievable?

It seems **Charlotte** is in denial of her circumstances. She hasn't really made good choices throughout her career, preferring to live in the present. Now is the time to decide what her future looks like. Instead of dreaming big, Charlotte needs to focus on what she has and what she can realistically expect to happen in the future. Starting now at least puts things in perspective.

Devise a strategy

Evaluate the most promising options for achieving your goals

Plan for contingencies

Remain flexible

Nobody expects to be widowed young. **Olga** certainly didn't. Going through the grief of losing her beloved Alexei and trying to figure out how to care for her family when she has no knowledge of where that money will come from will be the reason for her to sit down and devise what her short- and long-term goals will be. She always loved to care for her family. Perhaps finding an interesting cooking position or cleaning job will help her get back on her feet. She needs to develop a life plan as soon as possible and stick to it.

Beth, having been recently diagnosed with a slowly progressive multiple sclerosis, knows she has time to think about what she wants in the future. Her adult daughter and her parents are good family supports making it easier for her to manage her life changes. She still needs to look at short-, medium- and long-range goals before she tries to put her life plan in place.

Action Plan
By sticking to it, you will realize your dreams.

Look at it often

Evaluate it regularly

Update it when necessary (at least every three to five years)

Revise it as your situation changes

Most importantly, you need to find the right balance in your life. The ideal way would be to keep a journal. Write down what you think and how you feel about about your day-to-day life. Things can get out of hand very quickly, creating stress that can affect your health and outlook on life. Look at the entire picture, not just small chunks of it. There will always be times in your life when you feel overwhelmed. Take time to reflect on what you want to achieve. Revisit and update your life plan every three to five years.

Think positive! Plan well! Enjoy life! Make it work!

Update your dreams and goals, then create a place of action and go after them.
— Karen Hood-Caddy, Findhorn Book of Everyday Abundance

CHAPTER 3

You Belong to You

Age is an issue of mind over matter. If you don't mind, it doesn't matter.
— Attributed to Mark Twain

Facts:

1. The population of Canada is aging faster than ever before.

2. Chronic conditions happen throughout our lifetime. We learn to manage them with diet, exercise and medication.

3. People who remain socially active can live longer, healthier lives by increasing their level of physical activity, eating healthy food and taking steps to eliminate falls.

With an aging population, you could become a caregiver to a parent or other elderly person while still involved in an active career. Taking care of yourself is very important. Too often, siblings defer to a single sister to become the caregiver when it should be the domain of all.

Being single by chance, **Karima** has genuine concerns about who will take care of her in old age. She is socially active but has not made a decision on what friend she will ask about taking on a power of attorney for care. In the meantime, she must work on maintaining a healthy lifestyle to ensure she is able to live a rich, full life.

Caring for her parents is a concern for her. They live about two hours away from her, and although they are showing no signs of care needs right now, Karima knows she will be the one they call upon to assist them. She knows her brother will not be any help to her.

It may be necessary for Karima to call on friends and neighbours of her parents to assist her. There are government agencies and not-for-profit organizations as well as private agencies that provide help. She should find a support group when the time comes to provide that extra care to aging parents. *Don't try to do it all on your own, Karima!*

Charlotte recently developed cardiac symptoms that gave rise to stent implants. Her only living relative is a nephew in another city. On the other hand, **Olga** expects to be cared for by her children. This is the expectation in some cultures.

Consider the Impact of Life Stages

- **Reaching the end of our career**
- **Declining health**
- **Death of parents, friends and colleagues**
- **Children moving away**
- **The loss of independence**

What Aging Healthy Means
- Finding new things to enjoy
- Staying physically and socially active
- Adapting to change and feeling connected to community and loved ones

Change has hit **Samantha** hard. It is not what she expected, and it has affected every aspect of her life. She is very fortunate her parents were able to take her and her children in when she and Barry separated. Right now, she needs to focus on her own survival and ensuring her children's needs are adequately met. Diet, exercise and socializing are key factors in maintaining a healthy lifestyle.

For some, change brings anxiety and fear. How will I care for myself in later life because I have no children? Will I lose my mind? Don't let negative thoughts bog you down. Learn to laugh. Laughter enriches our lives. It is contagious and helps bring people together. It allows us to let go of our inhibitions and reservations, making us fun to be with.

Tips
- Be thankful for the things you have
- Share your feelings with friends
- Keep a journal
- Maintain a sense of humour (laugh out loud)
- Always look for the silver lining

- **Find meaning and joy in life**
- **Take risks**
- **Meet new people**

Charlotte is fortunate to have close friends who truly care about her. She needs to begin focusing on her future. However, getting her life back after the shock of losing her job has been difficult. She needs to continue to enjoy the companionship of others, find projects of interest to her or even take up a new language with a focus on new learning.

Suggestions
- **Find an activity that appeals to you**
- **Pick up an old hobby or find a new one**
- **Take a class or join a club**
- **Learn something new (a new instrument or foreign language)**
- **Enjoy an outing to a concert, an art gallery or museum**
- **Explore nature (walking, hiking, and biking)**
- **Take a trip to a place you have never been before**
- **Get involved in your community by volunteering**

Connectedness is very important at all stages of life but definitely more so when you no longer go out to work. If you have stopped working, start by putting your foot out the door each day. You never know what will be open to you on the other side. Those who have pets know the joy they bring to our lives and how helpful they can be when life doesn't seem worth living. Think about bringing a pet into your life. Yes, they are a responsibility, but, having a pet is a very rewarding experience.

Recently widowed, **Olga** might find it difficult to put her life in order after the death of Alexei. The funeral home put her in touch with a bereavement counsellor and gave her several copies of the official death certificate, which is always required as proof of death when applying for benefits.

It may be necessary for her to contact Alexei's former employer to find out if she can benefit from any pensions he may have contributed to as well as any insurance policies.

Beth needs to take care of herself. She is keen to add new people to her life, and by keeping her brain active, she hopes to ward off cognitive changes and memory problems. Keeping physically fit will help her face any future mobility issues. She needs to explore the organizations in her neighbourhood that provide programs and activities she might join where she will meet new people. She should focus on making positive changes to her own life.

Activities

- **Call up old friends and ask them to share time with you**

- **Keep in touch with close friends and family**
- **Meet one new person every week**
- **Locate a support group if needed**
- **Volunteer**
- **Join a meetup group (www.meetup.com/ca)**

As we age, everything starts to slow down: our metabolism, our sense of taste and smell, our vision and hearing decline. Our levels of activity move from go-go to slow-go (needing some assistance) to no-go (services brought to us). Thus, the need to take care of ourselves as we age. Here are some ways to do that.

- choose colourful fruits and vegetables and whole grains over processed food
- prepare meals from scratch that are tasty and visually appealing
- drink plenty of fluids to avoid dehydration.
- share a meal with someone

Fact: Staying healthy involves exercise. It improves mental health and can offer pain relief from chronic disease such as arthritis. Before you proceed with any exercise regime, check with your doctor first.

Samantha really needs to focus on staying healthy not only for herself but for her children as well. She has had to make many changes to her lifestyle as she picks up the pieces from her failed marriage and learns to cope with the road ahead.

Tips for Staying Healthy
- **Take a daily walk**
- **Find an activity you like and pursue it**
- **Join an age-appropriate exercise group**
- **Hire a personal trainer**

If you have difficulty sleeping at night and find you need a nap in the afternoon, don't worry, it's all right.

Relaxing at bedtime
- Turn off the computer and television an hour before retiring
- Keep noise levels to a minimum
- Keep the bedroom comfortable, quiet and dark
- Develop bedtime rituals such as a warm bath or quiet music
- Avoid extra liquids
- Try to go to bed at the same time every night

Tips
- **Join a book club**
- **Play board games such as Scrabble or Upwords**
- **Do puzzles**
- **Try new recipes—start a cooking group**
- **Learn a new skill**

Aging affects each and every one of us differently. Chronic illnesses may make it more difficult to change a bed, do laundry, find transportation to a doctor or dentist, or prepare a meal. Help is available from a variety of sources. Ask your family doctor for help: You might need a physician's referral to access services, but some services will be covered by your provincial health insurance.

Government support

Each province has its own rules and regulations about the amount of assistance it is able to provide to individuals. It is best to make direct contact in your area to learn what the provincial government can offer you.

- **Alberta www.health.alberta.ca/health-care-insurance-plan.html**
- **British Columbia www2.gov.bc.ca/gov/content/family-social-supports/seniors**
- **Manitoba www.gov.mb.ca/health/homecare/**
- **Newfoundland & Labrador www.health.gov.nl.ca/health**
- **New Brunswick www2.gnb.ca/content/gnb/en/departments/health.html**
- **Northwest Territories www.hss.gov.nt.ca/health/home-care**
- **Nova Scotia novascotia.ca/dhw/msi**

- Nunavut www.gov.nu.ca/health
- Ontario www.health.gov.on.ca/en/public/programs/ohip/
- Prince Edward Island www.healthpei.ca/home-care
- Quebec www.ramq.gouv.qc.ca/en/citizens/health-insurance/pages/health-insurance.aspx
- Saskatchewan www.ehealthsask.ca/HealthRegistries/Pages/health-benefits.aspx

Not-for-profit agencies can provide home help and personal care. They do charge for these services. However, if you are on a limited income, you may qualify to have the fees adjusted downward. To find these agencies, you could contact your local public health department or check government listings on the internet.

For-profit agencies are everywhere. Most of them offer personal support with some homemaking services for a specific hourly rate. Some of them will negotiate charges depending on how many hours of care are provided. They are listed in the Yellow Pages of telephone directories, and for those with access to a computer, they are online.

Things to Consider When
Using a Nursing Agency

- Who will provide the care (qualifications of care giver)?
- Do they have a contract with a personalized care plan?
- What type of training/supervision do they offer?
- How long has the agency been operating?
- What is covered in the hourly costs?
- How often do they invoice clients?

Often, a person will need help with bathing, dressing, grooming, and food preparation only. This can be provided by a personal support worker. It does not have to be a registered nurse. However, if a registered nurse is needed for wound care or other health care, they can be obtained through an agency or even your local government support system.

It is your life. Taking on new challenges can be risky. However, if you don't take risks, you cannot make change happen.

CHAPTER 4

Less Work, More Play

The boomers' biggest impact will be eliminating the term "retirement" and inventing a new stage of life...the new career arc.
—Rosabeth Moss Kanter, *Harvard Business Review*

What do you think life will look like for you when you are no longer working? Where will you be living? What hobbies and interests do you presently enjoy that you will still pursue? What new ones do you want to try? Are you interested in travel?

Leaving work can have both a practical and an emotional aspect to it. Looking at the practical aspect is like looking for a new job. Search out what you will do when you are no longer working before you stop working. Emotionally, it can take up to two years to get over leaving work if you have no plans in place. That gives depression room to set in, and it will slow down your acceptance of the idea that you are no longer working but need to find meaningful ways to fill your time.

Now that you have banned the word "retirement" from your vocabulary, it's time to re-*fire*. Think of it as transitioning from work. The rules have changed. For some, it is breaking free of a job they never liked anyway but stayed in for the benefits. If you do not have an appropriate financial portfolio established, you still may want to know what alternatives and options are available. If you enjoy what you do, you may want to continue working at the same position. It is a matter to be decided between you and your employer. Of course, you need to be happy and healthy and able to maintain the challenges of day-to-day expectations.

- Do you like to travel?
- What hobbies and interests can you pursue?
- Are you interested in part-time work?
- How about volunteering?
- Does higher learning appeal to you?

This may be the time to consider doing something you have always wanted to do. If you have a pension to fall back on, you might want to start your own business. Should you decide to start your own business, it may take three to five years to make it profitable. For others, it might be a time to travel to faraway places they have always dreamed of but didn't have the time to pursue. Think of this time of life as a permanent long weekend. How will you fill the time?

Women who broke the mould in the '60s are now at the age where they want to withdraw from work, and and in their transition from those high-paying, high-powered positions, they are really struggling to understand what the future means for them. For these women, it is truly a loss of identity. The daily routine is gone. There are no more meetings or staff crises to manage. Without addressing the future, it's easy to slip into a depression, and thus we see the importance of planning ahead.

Life is more than working for pay: People need to participate and become involved in social, civic, recreational, intellectual or spiritual pursuits throughout life. Being engaged in such pursuits provides a sense of fulfillment that in turn has a positive effect on health. It allows a flow of experiences that are intrinsically satisfying, imparting a sense of purpose and developing the opportunity for positive social relationships.

For **Charlotte**, leaving work was devastating. By not planning ahead, she put herself into a very vulnerable position that was not easy to manage on her own. Always have a backup plan.

Most people equate who they are with the work they do. When they are no longer working, it becomes very difficult to describe who they are. In reality, *you aren't who you think you are. It's: What you think, you are.*

Now is the time to prepare your answer, especially if you want to have business cards printed up. Look at all the positive things you like to do. Ignore the negatives

My name is _____. I am (a sister, aunt, friend). I like to (walk, bicycle, do crafts, swim, travel, eat out, read a good book). At present, I am reading _____.
I enjoy hiking, riding my bike, and travel. My favourite movie is_____. I belong

to (list the various clubs and organizations).
My dog/cat (name) is my faithful companion.

Add anything else you want without mentioning what you did in your career. Once you are comfortable with your new status, you could include what you did but only at the end. Maybe you can think of a catchy tagline to put on your business card. Remember, this is about *you* now. Practice using this format so when somebody asks who you are, you can tell them. Once you have that perfected, think about how you can re-define and redesign a business card that suits your new lifestyle.

Part-time work

Leaving work without a pension means you will be re-lying on your own savings plus government pensions. Finding part-time work to top up your finances might be the best way to go. However, if you like a particular aspect of what you do and feel it could be accom-plished on a part-time basis, ask your employer if they would be willing to keep you on in that role. Do not as-sume you can translate what you did into a consulting business without doing a lot of research into the matter. It takes three to five years to turn a new business into a profitable situation.

Becoming a widow at 54 was not what **Olga** ex-pected. Losing her husband suddenly has presented new financial challenges to her. As a stay-at-home mother who enjoys cooking, she could start by finding part-time work as a waitress or with a catering company. Once she is back in the workforce, she will have better opportunities to see what other options are available to her.

Volunteering

If you have an adequate pension, there are many ways you can enrich your life. Your knowledge and skill set provide a perfect backdrop to volunteering with a specific group or organization. It can be quite demanding, so it is best to pick an area that is of particular interest to you. Make sure you can commit to a certain amount of time each week or month. Treat it like taking on a project that you can commit to for only three to six months. If you like it, you may want to continue. Perhaps you feel there is a need to help underprivileged children, or troubled teens, recovering addicts or even older adults. Maybe you love art and could become a docent at your local art gallery.

Since **Karima** has not lost her desire to find a life partner, by volunteering at a not-for-profit group or organization, she might indeed meet the man she has always been looking for.

Is there is an area of your life you feel needs changing? Now is the time to make that change. Find the group that best fits your needs and become an active advocate.

Having recently been diagnosed with multiple sclerosis, **Beth** would be wise to get involved in her local Multiple Sclerosis Society. It would help her to better understand her diagnosis, and through volunteering, she could also help others.

If you join a group, a choir, a club or an organization, don't think of it as something you commit to for a long time. We should never make long-term commitments to anything. We can give our best for only a period of three to five years in any capacity, and then it is time to withdraw and let others take the helm, much like a rose blooms best when it is pruned back.

Higher learning

Many women who are currently working have never learned to knit, crochet or sew and have absolutely no interest in bingo. Many are professionals who have been involved in creative decision-making, doing sports activities and enjoying the arts in their spare time. They may prefer to look to colleges and universities for courses designed for the 55-plus crowd.

Enrolling in courses would be an excellent way for **Charlotte** to meet new people and enjoy learning at the same time. Just the act of getting out of the apartment is stimulating.

It is not unusual for older adults to go back to college or university to pursue a certificate or a degree. Some colleges and universities offer free tuition to those over 65. If you just want to audit a course, it can be very interesting and rewarding. Aside from the learning component, it's a perfect opportunity to meet new people while opening up new avenues of interest.

Registering in college courses could be a way for **Olga** to branch out and learn new things while also meeting new people who could offer her interesting work possibilities.

There is a variety of great courses available. Don't procrastinate in applying for something that appeals to you. There are huge demands for these programs and courses, and most are offered at a minimum cost. All colleges and universities have excellent programs for older adults.

Try to *avoid having too much time on your hands*. It allows you to become bored or start worrying about health issues, leading to frustration, loneliness and depression.

Women enjoy the friendships and camaraderie the workplace provides, and that is what they miss most when they are no longer working. Perhaps the best way to replicate that is to *create your own social network* when you stop working.

Facebook is a wonderful platform for social networking, connecting with past and present friends

- Be careful choosing who you pick as friends
- Don't brag
- Keep it for fun
- Remember: Anything you put on Facebook is there in perpetuity.

The Urge to Travel

Travelling alone can be a fun and exhilarating experience. You have the independence to go where you want to go and might even learn a bit more about yourself doing so.

Denmark's capital, Copenhagen, often scores high on lists of safe cities for single women travellers, but if you do your research and make sensible choices, you can have a fun vacation nearly anywhere....

Tips

- Research your destination. Use the Internet and purchase up-to-date travel books about your location. Do use it discreetly.
- Have a backup plan in case of sickness, loss of passport, money, credit cards, etc. Leave copies of all your documents back home in case you need that information. Arrange other ways of getting cash from your bank if your ATM card doesn't work.
- Travel light. Make certain you can take your luggage wherever you go—to a restaurant or toilet if necessary! Your luggage should be gender-neutral so you don't stand out to thieves looking for jewellery.
- Fit into the environment. Dress like the locals. You don't want to stand out in a crowd. Leave expensive jewellery behind. Don't flaunt your money.
- Beware of public Wi-Fi. Hackers and scammers are turning to public Wi-Fi to access private informa-

tion. Avoid sending or receiving sensitive data.

- **Make sex safe.** When the forces of nature are strong, you should have your own protection. Carry condoms if you think you might have sex.
- **Trust your instincts. If you feel something isn't right, it likely isn't.** It's best to meet people in public places to avoid uncomfortable situations.
- Many trains, planes and cruise ships provide travel for single women without charging a singles supplement. Travel agents know where to find those deals and are the best way to make travel arrangements.

Recommended websites:

www.adventurewomen.com

www.journeywoman.com

www.gutsywomentravel.com

www.todayswomantraveller.com

www.women-traveling.com

www.roadscholar.org

www.executiveclasstravelers.com/1/adventure_travel.htm

Live as if you were to die tomorrow. Learn as if you were to live forever.
— Attributed to Mahatma Gandhi

CHAPTER 5

Home Is Where Your Heart Is

Never make your home in a place. Make a home for yourself inside your own head. You'll find what you need to furnish it — memory, friends you can trust, love of learning, and other such things. That way it will go with you wherever you journey".

— Tad Williams, *Memory, Sorrow and Thorn*

Lifestyle determines where you will live: close to work or public transit, renting or owning are major considerations. Leaving work permanently means another shift in lifestyle. If you use a cane or walker or are in a wheelchair, accessibility is paramount.

If you live in a house: Can you afford to stay there? (Perhaps you still have a mortgage to pay as well as taxes, utilities and overall maintenance.) Is the house suitable to allow for aging in place? (Renovations can be costly.) These are factors to consider when you no longer go out to work. They are also reasons to look at all of your options.

The housing market is constantly changing. More and more builders are trying to attract the mature consumer. Communities for older adults where there is access to a golf course and a community centre with programs and activities are springing up in both urban and rural settings. The aging process can have a profound influence on where you choose to live.

Advice: Roy, a real estate agent, recommends staying in your own home as long as you can, and when you feel you need to sell, move into a rental space. No more grass cutting, no more snow shovelling, no more maintenance cares or concerns. A very wise decision!

Making the Right Choice

Home is people, not a place.
— Robin Hobb, *Fool's Fate*

Maintaining independence is of utmost importance to all of us. So many elements influence our choice of housing: income, access to public transportation, closeness to shops, physical mobility and, not to be forgotten, socializing. These all play heavily into where and how we cope with the aging process.

Sharing

Remember the '80s television show *The Golden Girls*, where four women lived together in Florida? Women who are used to a partner and are suddenly single might find it beneficial to do just that. Do you invite someone into your house or do you move in with someone else? Maybe a few of your women friends would like to find a place for all of you to share. Hire a housekeeper and a groundskeeper so nobody has to be responsible for all the upkeep.

Things to consider

- Neighbourhood (friends, doctor, dentist, hairdresser, library, groceries, transportation, favourite coffee shop)
- Pets (will they be welcome?)
- Gardening (will you miss digging in the dirt and a sense of accomplishment?)
- Accessibility (needing a cane or walker)
- Personal assistance (formal or informal)
- Safety and security are paramount
- Access to entertainment and other events
- Urban or rural
- To stay or to move

Remaining at Home: Renovate or relocate

Adapting your home: Safety and security should be the number one priority. To stay and renovate or to relocate are real choices to make. Remaining in your home can certainly extend your independence if you make these changes.

Generally

- Improve indoor and outdoor lighting
- Install double railings on all stairwells inside and out
- Consider a stair glide if you have a two-story house;
- Make sure your smoke and carbon monoxide alarms are working (they are good for only five

years and then need replacing)

- Remove excess electrical and telephone cords to prevent tripping
- Keep ample room for movement around all furniture
- Have arms on all chairs
- Ensure all door locks are secure
- Use lever-action door openers instead of knobs
- Remove scatter rugs on wood floors
- Make sure all floor surfaces are non-slip
- Install low-pile carpeting throughout your home
- Install an outside ramp to give easy access to your home

Bathroom

- Put grab bars or a pole in the tub/shower area
- Put a pressure balance, anti-scald faucet in the tub or shower area
- Make sure the bathroom door opens outward—a pocket door is best
- All electrical outlets should be ground fault protected
- Install a hand-held shower
- Install a raised toilet
- Install a bath seat in the tub with a tub mat for safety
- Remove the tub and replace with a walk-in shower and seat
- Use night lights

- Must be purchased outright (no mortgage)
- You will be living with peers

Some life leases are part of a larger campus that may include a retirement home and or nursing home providing access to programs and activities.

Purchasing a Condominium

- Benefits: Freedom from grass cutting and snow shovelling
- Warnings: Ensure there is a healthy reserve fund for major emergencies.
- Monthly fees could become expensive

Renting a Condominium or Apartment

- Benefit: Allows you to remain in the same neighbourhood
- Freedom from being a homeowner
- Can lock the door and go away for the winter
- Warning: Environmental issues (heating, cooling, bug infestation)
- Find out what type of security (concierge, camera or both)
- Can you count on the landlord for maintenance?
- For first-time tenants: You should become familiar with the Landlord and Tenant Act in your jurisdiction. Speak to other tenants in the building to learn how major issues within the building are managed.

A disadvantage is that you will become dependent on the landlord for minor repairs and maintenance.

Seniors Communities

- Benefits: Caters to the 55-plus age group
- Predominantly bungalows
- Near a golf course and tennis courts
- Recreation centre
- Warning: The problem is that as health deteriorates, there may be a need for more physical care that is not available in this type of a setting.

For those who do not want to live around children, this is an ideal solution.

Seniors' Apartments

- Benefit: May have some rent geared to income units
- Warning: Be aware a wait list can be long

It is a fact that in larger cities, there will be a long wait list for subsidized units. The development chains Amica and Revera which have many retirement homes, also offer rental apartments at market rents.

Some church groups build seniors' apartment buildings right next to their worship buildings. These facilities tend to be less expensive because they are not-for-profit. Many will have at least 25% subsidized units. Ask friends and neighbours about these places if this is what best suits your needs.

Retirement Homes

- **Benefits: Independent living with some care provided**
- **Offer a variety of accommodations ranging from full suites to semi-private and private accommodation**
- **Freedom from cooking, cleaning, and home maintenance**
- **Social programs and recreational activities are a great way to become involved in retirement living**
- **Costs are dependent on location and amenities**

Retirement homes come in all shapes and sizes. They are found in both urban and rural settings. The older retirement homes may have only a kitchenette because everyone is expected to eat in the dining room.

Many retirement homes coming onto the market today are apartments within a retirement setting. Each unit has a full kitchen for the resident, but there is the option of purchasing food in the dining room. Many have a bar, a spa, a pool and a library and offer art classes, book clubs, concerts, movies and organized outings. They really are like a mini community.

As we age, we become more dependent. Many retirement homes provide assisted living care floors where there is nursing staff to look after the changing needs of the residents. Some of the newer homes can provide care in each individual unit. The biggest issue to consider when more care is required is the increased cost. When searching out a retirement home that meets your needs, find out about the different levels of care offered and the different levels of fees for such care.

Long-Term Care

- **Benefits: Provides 24-hour nursing care with medical attention**
- **Help with bathing, grooming, dressing, toileting, eating**
- **Secured areas for people with dementia**

All long-term care homes are regulated by the province to meet specific standards (food, staffing, fire and safety)

Take time to visit facilities in your neighbourhood. Know and understand what they can provide. Talk to the residents. Ask the staff if they would put a loved one there. Become knowledgeable by asking lots of questions. Find out the procedure for making an application to a long-term care facility where you live. Each province determines the cost to the resident and is the regulator of all rules governing long-term care.

Making the Move

Regardless of age, any move is traumatic, whether around the block or to another city. It can be a very daunting experience particularly, if you have lived in the same place for a long time.

The hardest thing to accomplish once the decision to move has been made is to start **downsizing**. Time is paramount. The more time you have to do it, the better. Start small, with one room at a time. If it feels too overwhelming, hire professionals to help you downsize.

Ask for a floor plan of your new location. Measure the furniture you want to take with you to ensure it will fit.

What about pets? Will your new location accept pets? Pets are part of our family and play a huge role in our lives.

Beware: An attachment to things (precious items, heirlooms gathered over the years) can be a stumbling block to letting go. Take photos of your favourite items to put into an album before giving them up. That way you can look at them and reminisce any time without having them take up valuable space.

Lifestyles today are much more casual. The silver tea service that your mother so proudly displayed on the sideboard is no longer of use to you. The china and sterling silver flatware is never used anymore, but you still hang onto them. Now is the time to assess what you truly need. What you don't need, you can sell or give away to friends or relatives to donate to a charity, or you could even have a yard sale.

Appraisals: Use professionals to evaluate your

items. Selling appraisals are very different from insurance appraisals. It is always wise to use professionals to evaluate items so you get fair market value if and when you decide to sell.

Avoid storing! A cautionary note to those who think they may want items in the future: If you haven't used it in the past year, perhaps you really don't need it. If you are planning to leave items to friends and relatives, ask them now if they want these items and don't be disappointed if they decline. Finding people and places to take unwanted items can be difficult but is better than just putting the items into storage. Storage can be expensive.

Choosing a Mover

There are a number of moving companies across Canada that cater to older adults. These are professionals who understand the aging process and the need to downsize, and they can help you sort through years of accumulations . *Find out if they belong to the National Association of Senior Move Managers* www. nasmm.org). It is an American association with many Canadian companies as members.

Remember, you are most likely moving to a smaller space and therefore cannot take everything. These professionals are with you from the beginning to the end of the move.

Older adults are often reluctant to accept the help of a moving service that caters to them. They are convinced they can manage the sorting, downsizing and packing but in reality, they cannot. It is just too overwhelming for them. On top of that, they feel vulnerable and reticent about involving others. A moving service specifically for older adults can be a real godsend. They take the work and worry out of the move.

Movers do carry insurance, but if your items are important to you, you many want to contact your own insurance provider to cover them during the move.

Costs to consider: Consulting fees for the overall project management of the move.

Fees for valuating items no longer needed or wanted, downsizing, packing, moving, unpacking and setting up in the new location.

Remember to notify all utility companies, Canada Post, financial institutions, family and friends.

Final Considerations

Make a list of the pros and cons about your current living situation. Who else will be affected by your decisions, and does it matter? Location is important. The three things that older adults want most when they are no longer working are:

1. closeness to a cardiac unit,
2. closeness to public transportation and
3. closeness to higher learning.

Before making any final decisions about a move, speak to your financial advisor about costs and affordability.

"Home" in any language is an important word. It can mean many different things. In *The Wizard of Oz,* Dorothy's comment on home is probably one of the more famous and remembered uses of the word "home":

*Oh, but anyway, Toto. We're home–*home*!*
And this is my room–and you're all here –
And I'm not going to leave here ever, ever again,
because I love you all. And...oh, Auntie Em, there's
no place like home!

CHAPTER 6

Are You a Sandwich or a Hamburger?

Stuck in the sandwich generation is no baloney.
—Tavia Grant

When the matter of care giving to an older adult becomes an issue, balancing career and personal needs must be addressed. Are you a sandwich or a hamburger? An "open-faced sandwich" is someone who has aging relatives but no children. "Regular sandwiches" are those who are caught between aging relatives and growing children. A single woman caring for both children and parents from more than one previous marriage would be a "hamburger," with multi-layered generations to manage.

Facts:

- Baby boomers who are now caregivers will soon require care themselves.
- People are living longer, resulting in more debilitating illnesses later in life.
- Hospital stays are shorter—more care is needed at home.
- Women, traditionally the caregivers, are now in the workforce.

Care requirements of older people

Samantha, who is now living with her parents, may recognize changes occurring in them that might worry her. What will happen if her parents also need care while she is still working and trying to provide for her two children, Jessica and Sam? Now is the time for her to become aware of future needs her parents may have.

Personal care: bathing, dressing, toileting, grooming, feeding.

Other care needs: meal preparation, transportation, managing medications, coordinating services, communicating with healthcare professionals.

Managing the balancing act

- Evaluate the situation
- Assess how care needs can best be met
- Devise a plan
- Determine time management on caregiving tasks
- List all caregiving responsibilities–delegate to others
- Explore services and resources in the community
- Learn how to manage stress
- Stay healthy
- Join a support group
- Ask for help when needed
- Hire a geriatric care manager
- Discuss finances long before you think you should

Having that difficult conversation with parents should be done when everyone is able to remain calm, cool and collected. Listen to what your parents are thinking about their own aging issues and how it can affect you. Find out what medications they are on in case they get admitted to the hospital and they cannot remember. If there are other siblings, they too need to be brought into the conversation. If you are an only child, you may need to solicit the assistance of other family members or even friends and neighbours of your parents.

Since **Karima** does not live close to her parents, it would be wise to schedule a meeting with them to discuss their wants and needs as they age. Can they remain in the country setting where they reside? How close are they to medical care? What housing options are available to them? Will her brother be prepared to step in if necessary? Can he be counted on for help either physically or financially?

Dementia: a scourge of old age

Dementia care is a major concern. An inability to remember a name or place happens as we age. We all have moments of forgetfulness. However, when you lose your way home or forget important appointments, these can be signs of cognitive impairment and should be addressed.

To date, 38 different types of dementia have been recognized. "Dementia" is the term applied to a progressive, degenerative neurological condition that attacks the brain, resulting in memory loss and an inability to perform familiar tasks. It can also affect personality, language use and behaviour.

Alzheimer's disease is one form of dementia. Other forms include Lewy bodies, Parkinson's, frontal lobe dementia, and vascular dementia, which is dementia caused by strokes. If there is reason to suspect dementia is an issue, it is crucial to get a diagnosis as soon as possible when there are programs and activities to help manage the disease.

By 2031, 1.4 million Canadians will have dementia. Nearly one million of them will be susceptible to wandering.

New tracking devices such as a GPS SmartSole that fits inside a person's shoe are already on the market. The SmartSole discreetly tracks, monitors and locates the person with dementia. It may not be a cure, but it certainly is a helpful tool when caring for a person with dementia who is prone to wandering. At least it prevents the person from getting lost.

While some medications may slow the process down, none has proven effective in the long term.

Sticking to a familiar routine helps a person with dementia cope for longer periods. If it is customary to spend time in a southern climate during winter months, it could become a real concern for those with dementia, as it disrupts the daily routine. Cueing and giving simple direction is very useful. Activities such as walking, listening to music and being part of a group all help those who have been diagnosed with dementia.

Local Alzheimer Societies have information and referral services as well as support groups, programs and activities for people with dementia and educational programs for caregivers.

Driving is a privilege, not a right
Older people do not want to give up driving. They feel it is a loss of independence. Key signs that driving is an issue:

- **Dents in the car**
- **Driving at inappropriate speeds**
- **Confusing gas and brake pedals**
- **Hitting curbs**
- **Parking inappropriately**
- **Making poor judgement decisions on lane changes**

Today's aging population is already seeing massive changes to automobiles. Several automobile manufacturers have developed self-parking cars. Several automobile manufacturers have designed a way of notifying the driver when there is another car in a blind-spot. There is already evidence of a driverless car coming on the market soon. Communities are becoming more age-friendly and are addressing the need for better transportation so people are not reliant on their automobiles. We count on our cars to help us shop and get to appointments and events, making it difficult to give up this luxury.

Facts:

- One in 10 people over 65 years of age will develop dementia
- One in 5 people over 85 years of age will develop dementia
- One in 2 people over 90 years of age will develop dementia

Karima, **Beth** and **Samantha** have aging parents. **Beth** and **Samantha** are part of the sandwich generation, caught between their children and aging parents. For each of them, it would be wise to have that difficult conversation with their parents to find out what their parents envision for the future while still managing to organize their own lives. As their parents age, their cognitive and physical abilities may diminish. Will they want to remain in their own homes or will they willingly go into a care home? If they remain in their own homes, do their parents expect their daughters to be caregivers? Can they afford to hire help for personal care, meal preparation and maintenance?

These are the reasons it is best to have such a conversation while their parents are able, before that hip fracture occurs and it is too late.

If you are still working and become a caregiver to an aging parent or relative, you may spend an inordinate amount of time on the phone, while at work, trying to organize all the components required for caregiving.

This can be very stressful. How good are you at managing stress?

When you find caregiving is getting you down:

* Figure out what you can do about it
* Talk to a friend or colleague about your concerns
* Go to a movie or do something you enjoy
* Have a good belly laugh

There are both public and private agencies to assist you. Most are fee-based. Many will require a minimum session of four hours. If you need less, perhaps you can negotiate with the agency to meet your requirements. Local not-for-profit agencies can provide personal care and food preparation as well as home maintenance on a fee-for-service basis. They do not always require a minimum amount of time. The best way to locate them is to search online for those in your neighbourhood.

Do not hesitate to seek professional help by using an eldercare consultant who can help you navigate the complex, challenging health care system. *caremanagement.ca/find-a-care-manager.php* An eldercare consultant can also put a plan in place that will give both you and your loved one peace of mind.

CHAPTER 7

Dollars and Sense: It's Money, Honey!

Plans are nothing. Planning is everything."
— Dwight D. Eisenhower

It is often said that planning finances is more of a journey than a destination. Unlike science or math, creating a financial plan for your future offers many options. The major difference is that the path you choose will have everything to do with your unique set of circumstances.

Important things to remember on life's journey

- **There is no crystal ball**
- **Predicting the future is not easy**
- **Life happens!**
- **Create choices!**

Why Plan?

- To prevent failure
- To seek out alternatives
- To get the best results

Fact: More than 65% of Canadians do not have a financial plan. Considering the myriad of financial issues we will grapple with in our lifetime, this is troubling.

Think Positive: Focus on what you really want to

do and zero in on realistic goals. Most people spend more time planning a holiday than they do planning for retirement, but the process is the same.

Building a Thoughtful Retirement Plan

- Where do you want to go or what do you want your life to be like after you stop working?
- How will you get there or how will you reach your goals?
- When will you arrive at your destination or what specific date are you working toward?
- What will you do when you get there or how will you fill your time when you are no longer working?
- What might stop you from reaching your destination goals?

Keep in mind that retirement planning is like planning for a vacation that might last 30 years.

Financial Fact or Fiction? Life expectancy for Canadian men is 84. Life expectancy for Canadian women is 80. Answer: Fiction. Life expectancy is 84 for women. They outlive men by an average of four years.

The single women in this book have all been thrown a curveball. **Olga, Samantha** and **Beth** became **single by chance. Charlotte** and **Karima** are **single by choice.**

How well they cope depends on how well they deal with the challenges before them. They will need to think through a number of financial issues carefully in order to carve out a new path.

What will be the key to their success? Preparation....

What is a financial plan and how can it help me?

- **Captures financial information specific to your circumstances**
- **Helps you prioritize your goals and aspirations**
- **Includes strategies and timelines to help you reach your goals**
- **Addresses the hazards of your current situation and how to best deal with them**

Fact or Fiction? In order to have a financial plan I need to have some investments before I start. Answer: Fiction. You just need to have a vision of what you want for the future to start your financial plan.

A well-thought-out plan can be a useful tool to help you think through a number of "what if" scenarios that could happen during your lifetime.

Charlotte has enjoyed her life and does not seem to have a budget or keep track of her spending. How might this habit affect her in the long term? She may outlive her assets.

Are you in control of your cash flow or is it in control of you?

Ask Yourself:

- Do you know how much you need to pay the bills each month?
- Are you saving a portion of your income to create income down the road?
- Will it be enough to provide for you?
- Do you have funds on hand to deal with an emergency, job loss or a large unexpected expense?
- Do you have your debts under control?
- Do you have access to reasonable borrowing rates should you need credit?

Did You Know? A budget will help you to stay on top of how you spend your money.

- Create a budget to see where you stand financially
- Start by writing down your expenses
- Measure your expenses against the income you have coming in
- Put a system in place to track your spending such as using cash only for discretionary expenses

---

Responsible Ways to Use Your Credit Card

- Big-ticket items
- Online shopping
- When buying airline tickets and travelling

- **For reward programs to stretch your dollar further**

Remember to pay your credit card on time. Late payments will reduce your credit score and lead to the vicious cycle of borrowing at higher interest rates.

Did You Know?

A high credit score (700 or more) gives you access to the lowest borrowing rates available. Don't be afraid to negotiate with your bank for lower interest rates on your credit cards, loans or lines of credit. Keep in mind that the all the banks are competing for your business when you have good credit.

In case of an emergency

- **A line of credit can be used to pay for unexpected expenses at significantly lower interest rates than credit cards**
- **Set up a line of credit long before you need it**
- **Plan to have three to six months of cash on hand for a rainy day**
- **Commit to saving 20% of your income now for future cash flow**
- **Keep in mind that the future happens even to those who don't plan**

Life Insurance: What do I need to know?

Single by chance, **Samantha**, who is newly divorced, never thought she would need to worry about having life insurance to protect her family. **Olga**, who is recently widowed, never really thought about the financial impact of losing her husband, Alexei, who was the breadwinner.

What will you do if life does not turn out the way you imagined?

Have a contingency plan for the people who rely on you financially. Ensure your contingency plan addresses the financial impact a spouse's or ex-spouse's death or disability would have on you and your children. Find a competent advisor to help you get the right coverage in place.

Can you really afford to wait?

A TD *Risky Business* poll revealed that a majority of Canadians claim to be cautious and risk-avoiders (55%), with only 8% saying they are risk-takers. However, the same poll found that three in ten Canadians don't have life insurance and six in ten don't have critical illness insurance.

I am a single woman without children. Do I need to think about life insurance?

The short answer is "maybe." Single by choice, **Karima** and **Charlotte** may not feel they need to think about life insurance since they do not have heirs to worry about.

Ask yourself: How will my final expenses be paid? Will those left behind be able to access those funds?

Do the math: Pre-plan your funeral arrangements and compare the costs of paying out of pocket versus buying insurance. Have a will in place to ensure your executor knows your wishes. Consider that the funds in your bank account may be tied up until the estate settles, leaving your executor to pay the costs while waiting to be reimbursed by your estate. Would you want to leave your executor in this position?

Financial Fact or Fiction? If I die in debt my heirs are responsible for my debts. Answer: Fiction. Your heirs are responsible for your debts only if they signed for the debts as well. On the other hand, depending on the contract, spouses can be sued by a creditor for their deceased spouse's debts.

Living Benefit Insurance: What do I need to know?
Critical illness insurance: Pays a one-time tax-free lump sum upon diagnosis of a critical illness such as cancer, heart attack or stroke. Most plans cover 21 major illnesses. The amount of coverage can range from $5,000 to $1 million of coverage, 30 days after being diagnosed with a major illness.

How can this plan benefit you? Should you be diagnosed with a major illness, critical illness insurance can help pay for lifestyle expenses as you recover and for treatments not covered by your provincial health plan. It can also pay off or pay down mortgage debts so you can focus on recovering from your illness.

Disability insurance: Pay up to 75% of your salary

if you are unable to perform the major duties of your occupation until the age of 65. The income can be tax-free if you paid for the policy yourself, or will be taxable if your employer paid for your plan.

Did You Know? The major differences between disability and critical illness plans?

Critical illness pays a onetime lump sum benefit, while disability pays a monthly ongoing benefit until age 65. Critical illness helps to protect your lifestyle. Disability addresses your ongoing needs for income if you are unable to work.

Single by choice, **Karima**, who is a business owner, has not yet thought through what would happen to her lifestyle if she became critically ill and was no longer able to run her business. A critical illness plan would give her the option to pay off her mortgage, and a disability plan would allow her to receive 75% of her income tax-free until retirement if she became permanently disabled.

Single by chance, 58-year-old **Beth**, who is separated, has a sizeable locked-in pension with her employer. However, she still has eight years until retirement. She should investigate what disability benefits are available to her, especially since she was recently diagnosed with multiple sclerosis. A disability plan will protect the income she earns until retirement.

Long-term care insurance: Pays for the costs of

care if you are unable to do two of the five "activities of daily living"(ADLs) or you lose your cognitive function. The ADLs include: feeding, dressing, bathing, transferring positions and using the toilet on one's own.

How can this plan benefit you?

A long-term care plan can help you to pay for the costs of care down the road should you lose your independence and want to receive care in your home or need cash to pay for the costs of care in a long-term care facility.

Ask Yourself: If you are a single without children have you considered how you will pay for care down the road if you need it? Will the government be able to provide all the care you may need?

If you are single with children, will your children be able to afford to take time out from their own lives to care for you? Would you want to them to?

Single by choice, **Charlotte**, has not fully prepared for retirement after receiving an early buyout package. She also does not have family support other than her nephew, to whom she is not that close. Should she lose her independence in the future, a long-term care plan will mean a close friend can step in and manage her care. It may also prevent her retirement nest egg from running out before the end of her life.

Single by chance, **Beth** and **Olga** may expect their

children to care for them should they lose their independence in the future. Some cultures have this expectation. Their children may want to consider purchasing long-term care insurance to have the funds needed to either care for their mom directly (some plans plan pay a monthly income) or hire someone to care for their mom if necessary.

Did You Know? According to Sun Life Financial (2015), it can cost over $2,500 per month to stay in a long-term care facility. Costs for private care vary widely, between $20 and $30 per hour for homemaking, personal or nursing care.

Choosing an Insurance Advisor

- **Ask for referrals**
- **Know the difference between a broker and an agent**
- **Find out if they have other credentials that may be helpful to you**
- **Check out their websites**
- **Finding a knowledgeable and trustworthy advisor is paramount**

Did You Know? An insurance agent represents one company and can offer only insurance solutions from the insurance company they represent. A broker represents a number of insurance companies and can offer solutions from the various companies they represent.

Investing for the Future: What's the Big Deal?

Consider this. The later you get to the party, the sooner it will be over. If you enjoy going to a dinner party, you know you will miss out on a lot if you get there late. This could mean missing out on good conversation, the last of the good wine or the last of the delectable food. Everyone wants to get to a party on time—not too early, but definitely not too late.

This holds true for investing as well. The earlier you start to save, the more investments you will have available in retirement and the easier it will be to save for your retirement goals. You need to put away a lot less the earlier you start. Commit to saving on a regular basis. It becomes more difficult to save as time goes on.

A woman who wants to build a secure financial future ensures that she pays herself first—as soon as she begins to earn an income.

Financial fact or fiction? If I start investing $200 per month at 20, will I have more funds than if I start investing $500 per month at 40, assuming I want to retire at 65? Answer: Fact. Yes, you will.

The lesson: Start as early as possible!

Single-by-choice **Charlotte** lost money in the markets in 2008. She is not sure if her finances will ever recover from this. On the other hand, single-by-chance **Beth** has been very careful with her money and accumulated a significant nest egg in her locked-in accounts with her employer.

Investment Returns and Expectations—Projected versus actual

- **Women tend to be more conservative investors than men**
- **Women are more likely to invest in products that are guaranteed, such as GICs**
- **Women worry about losing the initial amount that was invested**
- ***It's your money and your life—take control, and get informed!***

Did You Know? At age 65, life expectancy is 18 years for men and 20 years for women. Approximately 30% of women will survive to age 90.

Understanding Investments—An Advisor Can Help.

Ask yourself: How far away am I from retirement? What have I earned to date on my investments? How much income will I have in retirement?

Consult a Trusted Advisor Who Can:

- **Help you work out a realistic investment plan**
- **Strike a balance between taking too little or too much risk**
- **Help you factor in worst-case scenarios**
- **Ensure that you are saving enough to meet your retirement goals**
- **Offer investment products with proven track records**

Finding the Right Financial Advisor

How do they earn their money?

Some advisors get paid a commission. Others receive an annual rate based on the client's portfolio. This fee rate is agreed upon in advance of taking the client. Do your homework. Ask how the Commissioned Advisor will add value if they are paid a large up-front fee. For Fee advisors, confirm the fee is in line with industry guidelines for the size of your portfolio.

Can experts predict where stocks are headed?

Nobody knows whether stock markets will rise or fall in any given year. Beware of advisors who make promises that sound too good to be true. They are.

Can I see a sample portfolio?

This will help you better understand how the financial advisor will manage your portfolio. This means stressing the importance of asset allocation, diversification and rebalancing.

What credentials do they have?

The Certified Financial Planner designation is the most rigorous, showing intellectual competence, a subscription to a code of ethics, and an integrated fiduciary standard. It also ensures the advisor is committed to their profession.

Be wary of top advisor lists.

They rank assets under management. Advisors should be ranked by the experience they deliver and the unique strategies they are able to create for clients. The focus should be on the value these firms provide for clients, not their asset size.

Is the advisor walking the walk?

Ask the advisor how they track their own financial journey. Do they set goals and live within their means? How are they investing for their future?

Do you know what a CFP designation is? The Certified Financial Planner (CFP) designation (CFP) is a professional certification recognized in 26 countries around the world.

Taxes—Don't Pay More Than Your Fair Share

"Thinking is one thing no one has ever been able to tax."
—Charles Kettering, founder of Delco

Taxes are a fact of life in Canada, but often we have no

choice on how much tax we pay. Plan to pay less tax now: You still have some control of the amount of income tax you pay. Work with a competent tax professional, and get the tax credits you deserve today.

Did You Know? Areas of the tax law change when the federal and provincial governments pass their respective budgets each year. You need to keep track of the tax rules to ensure you are not paying more taxes than you need to. Find a good tax preparer to help you reduce your annual tax bill.

Plan to pay less tax later: What kind of taxes will you be paying in retirement? What can be done to reduce this bill? How can you prevent "Old Age Security clawback"? How can you enjoy as much tax-free income as possible?

Fact: To avoid a larger tax bill, it is important to get a picture of where your income will be coming from now and in retirement.

Work with a trusted advisor and accountant who can help you figure out your tax bill in retirement, look at strategies to prevent Old Age Security clawback and look at strategies to reduce your income tax bill now and in retirement.

Single by chance: Could it happen to you?
"Although divorce rates for most age groups
have been falling, silver separation is on the
rise. Many long-term marriages are falling on
the rocks of the daily grind, the empty nest, the
other lover or the reality of parallel lives that
do not touch."
— retirehappy.ca

Samantha and **Beth** never thought they would leave their relationships. **Olga** never imagined she would become a young widow. What steps could they have taken to improve their chances of financial recovery? They could have been more involved in financial decisions.

Ask Yourself

- **How involved are you with the financial decisions of the household?**
- **Are smart decisions being made with your family's resources?**
- **Are you prepared to make financial decisions on your own?**
- **Do you have basic financial knowledge and would you be willing to learn if you had no other option?**
- **Are there people you could call upon to help you?**

Think about your future! Commit to educating yourself about finances, and get out of your comfort zone.

Did You Know? The average age of a woman becoming a widow is 56 and yet much of the retirement information published is aimed at couples.
retirehappy.ca

Single by choice: Create the life you imagined.

Karima would like to have a partner but is enjoying living life on her own terms. **Charlotte** enjoys singlehood and lives her life to the fullest.

Financial fact or fiction? According to *Money-
sense*, most singles have to save a higher per-
centage of their income for their retirement than
couples. Answer: Fact

Ask Yourself

• **Are you a single woman with no plans to marry?**
• **How will you save for retirement on one salary?**
• **What can you do to improve your earning power?**
• **What are you doing to improve your financial
  awareness?**

Create choices! Start building your life plan now.
Don't wait: Look for the **opportunities** in your financial circumstances. Be flexible. This is a great time to
start a business. Get educated—congratulate yourself
for reading this book. Commit to being a lifelong
learner on the subject of personal finance.

> **Did You Know?** Women receive significantly lower retirement benefits than men. This is because women tend to earn less income than men and take time off to have and care for children and to care for aging parents.

What can be done to boost my retirement income?

Single-by-choice **Karima** rents out some of her home for income. This is an excellent strategy to boost income in retirement and obtain long-term financial security.

Single-by-chance **Olga** may want to consider starting a catering business to help pay the bills in retirement. Many women start businesses to reinvent themselves and to help pay for their retirement expenses.

> **Fact:** Women are living longer than ever. If the investments we purchase do not grow enough, our assets may run out before we die.

What money memories are you creating and leaving behind?

What is a money memory? It is a financial habit, example or philosophy learned often by observing how your parents managed money.

Ask Yourself

- Were my parents big spenders or savers?
- What were my parents' values about money?
- Did I inherit these values?
- Have they helped me become a better or worse money manager?

Olga and Alexei scrimped and saved to give their children everything, and now Olga is on her own, living with her adult children, on a reduced income. It is not clear if her children will be in a position to help her with paying bills and holding onto their home since they are sporadically employed and are not yet financially self-sufficient.

Have Olga's children, Lina and Dimitri, learned any lessons about money? Of course not! They are likely still expecting their mother to continue to care for them even though she is no longer financially able to do so. They still have a lot to learn. If you have children, share with them your financial situation to make it easier for everyone.

Did You Know? Last year, 28% of American adults told the National Foundation for Credit Counselling that they primarily learned personal finance from their parents. Among kids currently ages 8 to 14, 65% say they learn more about money from their parents than they do at school, according to a T.

Rowe Price survey released last month. (CNBC.com, April 2015)

The lesson: Aim to be a good financial role model not only for yourself but for the people you leave behind.

Single-by-chance **Samantha** has learned some financial lessons the hard way and now wants to carve out a brighter future for her children. She mentioned that she does not want her children to make the same mistakes she did.

What you can do to become a better financial role model for your children?

- Become more aware of the financial legacies you inherited—the good, the bad and the ugly—and decide if they are helping you take control of your finances
- Mentor your children in the areas of finance you feel you are good at such as budgeting or managing credit
- Get help in the areas of finance you are not literate in such as understanding investments, risk and returns
- Invite your children to participate in household money conversations such as managing needs vs. wants and saving for a rainy day

- **Don't shield your children from money conversations**
- **Commit to becoming more financially literate and helping your children become more money savvy as well**

Creating Your Financial Team

A single lady approaching retirement has lots of financial issues to consider. Think about creating a financial plan to get a big picture to look at your situation. A Certified Financial Planner can provide you with a written plan that will take into consideration your current investments, assets and debts, and make recommendations to improve your overall financial situation to help you reach your goals.

Did You Know? A financial advisor can have an insurance license, investment license or both. However, not all financial advisors hold the CFP designation. Find out which licenses your advisor has and which are most relevant to your current needs for advice.

Do your homework
- **Ask for referrals from friends and family**
- **Ask the planner to provide you with recommendations**
- **Ask for samples of their work**

- **Is it fee only? Commission only? Or a combination of both?**
- **What are the drawbacks and advantages of their compensation structure?**
- **Can they clearly state how they add value?**
- **How long have they been working as an advisor?**
- **Can they provide references from clients like you that they have worked with?**
- **What other licenses do they hold?**
- **What type of communication will you receive?**
- **How often will you receive statements about your investments?**

Finanical Fact or Fiction?

The majority of Canadians do not have a will. Answer: Fact. This means that many single women will pass away without a will.

Create Your Team of Professionals

- **Financial planner**
- **Accountant**
- **Real estate agent**
- **Retirement consultant**
- **Mortgage consultant**
- **Insurance advisor**
- **Eldercare consultant**

Look at your situation from every angle and get all

of your important questions answered.

Adovocate for Yourself or find a financial professional who can advocate for you.

CHAPTER 8

Can I Still Do It?

We don't see things as they are. We see things as we are.

— Anais Nin, quoting the *Talmud*

Yes, you can. Sexuality is not defined by the person you have sex with. It is about how you feel and how you choose to identify yourself. Sex embraces biological, physical, emotional and spiritual aspects of life. It is a sense of belonging. Most importantly, sexuality is diverse and deeply personal.

Becoming a widow also means losing the intimacy that goes along with marriage. For **Olga**, who is still in her 50s, the love of a husband no longer exists, leaving a void in her life. The same goes for **Beth** and **Samantha**, recently separated.

The physical or emotional aspect of sex is the bond between individuals expressed through feelings of love and trust. Spiritual sexuality refers to our connectedness to others. It involves issues or morality, ethics, theology or religion. Sexuality embraces all the senses. The simple pleasure of enjoying one's own body is sexual. Sexuality is a basic need in human experience. It is an important part of health.

Defining Sexuality

Straight: attracted mostly to people of the opposite sex or gender

Gay: attracted mostly to people of the same sex or
    gender (term used by men)
Lesbian: attracted mostly to people of the same sex
    (term used by women)
Bisexual: attracted to both men and women
Asexual: not really sexually attracted to anyone

Being single does not mean you can't enjoy sex. Some people say having sex is like riding a bicycle, as in "first, you need one." They mean a partner, but things have changed. Dr. Ruth says, "Use a vibrator but finish with a finger. Never, ever have an orgasm using only a vibrator." She is cautioning against becoming dependent on a vibrator to have an orgasm.

Society may think that older women do not enjoy sex anymore. Not true. Even single women like **Charlotte** have desires. Perhaps they don't always have a partner, but that doesn't rule out masturbation.

Fact
    The vagina shortens and narrows as we age with the walls becoming thinner and stiffer.

Solution
    Use a vaginal lubricant.

Remember
    It's O.K. to masturbate. Researcher Shere Hite's study (2003) found that four out of five women do it.

Some single women may still want to have sex and are willing to have a relationship with a man but without the ties. They relish their freedom and choose to remain single but with the benefits of enjoying a sexual experience. We all have personal choices.

Separated and divorced women like **Beth** and **Samantha**, who have enjoyed a happy, successful life, do not have to wait until they find another partner. An orgasm from masturbation is like buying shoes from Payless. Once you get the first pair, you get the second for next to nothing. If it feels good and it isn't breaking any law or hurting anyone—just DO IT!

People with disabilities have the same wants and desires as other people, yet are too frequently treated as non-persons. It is even more difficult for those who live in long-term care homes.

Despite staff efforts to provide a degree of privacy, a long-term care home is a difficult place to call home. A person's self-determination and freedom of action are too often denied by others—including their right to sexuality. Those with varying types of debilitating illnesses living in long-term care homes still have a desire for sex, love and touch.

Beth, separated and recently diagnosed with multiple sclerosis, is equally entitled to a happy, healthy, sexual existence. One day she may end up in a care facility. Hopefully the staff will be wise enough to understand all her needs, sexuality included, and give her privacy to enjoy whatever feels good.

Getting older doesn't mean your basic needs change.

One does not need to be old to understand that we all benefit from touch. It is a basic desire. That is why just the act of cuddling without the need for intercourse is important. Keep condoms handy if you plan to have penetrative sex. Because of increased sexual activity in the 50-plus age range, sexually transmitted diseases in older people have doubled in a decade. (*British Medical Journal*, 2013).

Karima is still looking for her Mr. Right. To be on the safe side when it comes to sexual health, she should always have a supply of condoms at the ready.

Wisdom gets stronger with age. Choose the road that best meets your needs and embrace the future with gusto.

CHAPTER 9

The Law Always Has Its Say

"Planning is bringing the future into the present so you can do something about it now."
– Alan Lakein

Who will make decisions for you when you no longer can? What guarantee do you have that the decisions made will be those you would have made for yourself had you been able? How would you like your property and assets distributed after you die? Who will be responsible? What assurance do you have that your wishes will be honoured? You may leave your family members and loved ones with more questions than answers. Thus, there is a real reason to have a well-crafted plan in place now.

The ladies highlighted in this book are women with different and varied life experiences, who would likely need or want different plans for their retirement, their estate and end-of-life decisions. Engaging the help of professionals such as a lawyer, an accountant, a financial advisor and even an elder care manager will ensure your specific needs are met.

Know what might happen. Be armed with essential information.

Powers of Attorney for Personal Care and Property

A **will** speaks for you from beyond the grave. A **power of attorney** speaks for you from your hospital bed.

A power of attorney is a legal document that identifies the author who will continue writing your story when you are no longer able. It assures you will be remembered for your accomplishments. A power of attorney is a key part to any estate plan and needs to be reviewed and updated regularly. Not having a power of attorney is risky, and may result in someone you do not want, or even the government, managing your finances. The person chosen must keep accurate records of all transactions.

Things you need to consider when drawing up a Power of Attorney:

- Who takes care of finances and paying bills?
- Who decides what happens to your home or personal belongings?
- Who chooses when you need to see your doctor or dentist?
- Who determines the level of medical care you will need?
- Who makes decisions about shelter, health, hygiene, nutrition and medical treatments?
- Do you want to have care provided at home or are you willing to go into a care facility?

Most jurisdictions in Canada have detailed legislation regarding the duties and responsibilities of an appointed attorney. Should you lose your mental capacity without a power of attorney, it may require a court order to enable someone to handle your affairs.

Karima, single without children, has a tenuous relationship with her brother. She is reluctant to ask her friends to take on this role. What happens if she gets into an accident and is mentally incapacitated before appointing her power of attorney? The longer she puts off appointing her attorney, the riskier it becomes.

Like Karima, **Charlotte** has no children and has not chosen an attorney yet. Luckily, she does have close friends who would be likely to take on the role, but she needs to see a lawyer to put that into place.

Power of Attorney for Property

The person you choose will be looking after all your financial affairs *if* you become mentally incapacitated, so you must choose a person that you trust implicitly. Integrity, honesty and willingness are the characteristics you must consider. The person you choose should be younger than you, adept at handling financial matters and someone who understands your wishes. A power of attorney for property is used when the person giving that authority is unable to act or make their own decisions. You may choose to build into your legal document that it can only occur when a doctor designates you incapable; otherwise it can be enacted at any time. Consideration must be paid to where this person resides. Preferably, it should be someone who lives nearby.

Currently more than 500,000 Canadians live with

dementia, and every year that number increases.

Given the likelihood that you will require assistance with decision making at some time in you life, it is far wiser to have a power of attorney in place to protect your best interests and honour your wishes when you are no longer able. Be aware, however, that without restrictions a power of attorney can be used at any time.

Mental Capacity

It is quite possible for a person to be incapable in one area and yet quite able to make decisions in another. It may be possible for you to make your own health decisions while having diminished ability to make financial decisions. You may be capable of deciding where you want to live but not able to manage your day-to-day finances, or when it comes to personal care, you may be able to make hygiene and shelter choices but not treatment decisions. The determination of capacity for making a will is similar to that as for making a power of attorney.

It is the lawyer's duty to the best of their knowledge and ability to make such an assessment as to whether the person has the capacity to give a power of attorney or make a will. If there is any doubt, it could be contested in court at a later date. A well-crafted power of attorney by a lawyer will allow for these variations. The legal age in most provinces to take on a power of attorney is 18 years and older.

To make a power of attorney for property, you must have the mental capacity to do so. That involves:

- **Knowledge of the kind and value of your property**
- **Awareness of obligations owed to your dependents**
- **Knowledge that your attorney will be able to act on your behalf**
- **Knowledge your attorney must fully account for all their dealings with your property**
- **Knowledge that if capable, you can revoke the power of attorney at any time**

A single woman without children may choose a relative or close friend to be her attorney. However, if your financial affairs are complicated, you may consider appointing a professional accountant, financial planner, lawyer or trust company as a co-attorney. Choosing an alternate who can act when the original is unable is a prudent measure.

Both **Olga** and **Beth** have adult children but this may not be the best solution. However, **Beth**'s only child is a first-year law associate at a large law firm so likely has the requisite skills and trustworthiness to handle the job. **Samantha**'s children are too young to be eligible. Being in an acrimonious divorce she has no spouse to choose for her attorney, so she needs to start looking to other relatives or good friends with the required skills and desire to assist.

Power of Attorney for Personal Care

Choose someone whom you are confident will make the same decisions for your care as you would have made for yourself. Your power of attorney for care will frequently need to consult with your property power of attorney for financial considerations. Problems can arise when your attorney for care seeks the best situation for you, but your attorney for property is overly protective of your assets. It is the duty of both attorneys to act in your best interest and in accordance with your wishes.

It is best to give specific instructions (some jurisdictions refer to a "living will" or "advance directive") with such a document, providing directions for carrying out your wishes about medical intervention, for example.

Becoming a power of attorney for personal care can be quite daunting and time-consuming. You might want to build in a form of compensation to cover the time and expenses encountered by your power of attorney for personal care.

In addition to having a power of attorney for personal care, you may also provide specific instructions to ensure you receive the medical care you want if you are terminally ill. "**Do not resuscitate**" is an example in certain cases, while in others you may want every possible measure to keep you alive. To better understand your choices, it is wise to have a discussion with your doctor before seeing your lawyer.

Risks Associated with Power of Attorney Documents

- Choosing the wrong person—they must understand the responsibilities and have the skills to make decisions on your behalf
- Appointing attorneys jointly—it is better done jointly and severally to avoid conflicts over care or property decisions
- If you appoint a specific child, it may upset other children, and/or they may not be able to accept the duties and responsibilities of an attorney

Staying Out of Harm's Way

Abuse comes in three forms: financial, physical and emotional. All three forms can be quite undetected unless someone "blows the whistle." Older people may become dependent on a child, a housekeeper, a friend or a neighbour who starts to take advantage of their diminishing cognitive skills. For example, if you give another person a power of attorney or put that person in charge of your banking or jointly on your bank account without restrictions, that person can remove all your assets without your knowledge or approval.

Caregivers and even family members or friends may resort to physical or emotional abuse to force someone to either provide them with financial support or have them put into the will so they will inherit everything.

Some cases of abuse or neglect may be the result

of stress on an attorney who is not equipped to take on the role.

These are the reasons it is imperative you pick the right person to act on your behalf when you are no longer able to do so.

Factors to consider when selecting an estate trustee:

Taking on the role of executor can be a very daunting task: dealing with accounts and finances, providing even-handed treatment of beneficiaries and knowing the deceased well enough to carry out their instructions. The person you choose as your executor will need to deal with all your property, both assets and liabilities. The size and complexity of your estate may dictate that you use a professional to act as a co-executor. An executor must be able to handle serious responsibilities governed by ethics and legal obligations.

Your Bequests and Legacies

Single women without children, like **Charlotte** and **Karima**, will need to carefully craft how they want their estate divided. Do you have other relatives to whom you want to leave a gift? Do you have a favourite charity? Who will inherit your property? Are there other people or organizations to whom you want to leave a final gift?

Single women like **Olga** and **Beth,** who have children, may still want to grant part of their estate to a charity or other organization. There is nothing to state you must leave everything to your children.

Being legally prepared means having well-thought-out powers of attorney, a will, and estate planning in place. It is far too easy to procrastinate. *Do it now.* Revisit it every few years or if changes occur in your life.

Remember, you are the author of your own destiny.

CHAPTER 10

Exit: Stage Right or Left? Your Choice

In this world, nothing can be said to be certain, except death and taxes.
— Ben Franklin

Life has a beginning and an end. As much as many of us want to bury our heads in the sand when it comes to discussing death, it is reality and requires discussion.

Ads for anti-aging products designed to help you feel better and live longer, whether food supplements or topical creams and ointments bombard you daily in print and social media. The term "anti-aging" is an oxymoron. We are aging from the moment we are born. It happens to all of us. How we embrace it is the issue. There is an end to it all, and that is a very good reason to consider pre-planning for the inevitable.

Different cultures have differing views on death and dying. Many feel if they do not discuss it, it will not happen. Others are just uncomfortable talking about dying.

To help you with those discussions, here are some facts about funerals.

Preplanning Your Funeral

Advantage: It spares those left behind the burden of making detailed decisions when they have nothing to fall back on.

Create a Plan

- **Put your wishes on paper**

- **Share this information with your executor**
- **Visit the preplanning consultant at the funeral home**
- **You may choose to prepay your funeral**
- **Advise your lawyer and financial planner**

If full payment is made, the funeral home puts the funds into a GIC that will bear interest with the assumption interest will accumulate enough to cover the overall cost at the time of death.

Did You Know? A funeral is not guaranteed until it is paid in full. If a person who is pre-paying a funeral dies before full payment is made, the estate is responsible for paying the difference. However, an insurance policy will ensure this doesn't happen.

In today's world, funeral pre-planning is a very competitive business. Therefore, it is wise to investigate the various options that are available to you. It is also recommended that you speak to your financial advisor to consider what is best for you.

Cremation

- **A preferred choice for some**
- **Requires legal authorization to the funeral director**
- **The funeral director completes the application**
- **Funeral director provides registration of death**

- **Remains are placed in a plastic container**
- **Remains can be transferred to a purchased urn for burial**
- **Find out where your remains can be legally placed**

In Ontario, there is a minimum waiting time of 48 hours after death before the cremation can take place. Each province has its own laws pertaining to this issue.

Burial

- **Can take place anytime after the death certificate is issued**
- **Registered with the municipality**
- **You must purchase a plot with a deed**
- **Requires a casket or container, which can be brought in or supplied by the funeral home**
- **You may want a vault for protection from the elements**

Sometimes the deed for a plot is lost or misplaced. If this happens and it is known what cemetery was chosen, the cemetery will have records of ownership. The size of the plot determines how many people can be buried in it.

Funeral services

- **Format determined by faith and culture**
- **Religious ties may require a church service**

- **Secular gathering may occur at a funeral home, club or organization**
- **A memorial service or event may occur days or weeks after death**

The format of the memorial or funeral event is usually stated in the deceased's will.

Some people want an elaborate religious ritual, others want a simple graveside departure. If you are called on to organize a funeral and there is to be no clergy present to run the event, then, use a master of ceremonies to keep things in check.

When leaving instructions for what's to happen after your death, remember to include your financial planner and your lawyer through all stages of planning.

Nobody knows how many years we have still ahead of us. Doing the right thing now about your end-of-life wishes means your last gesture to your loved ones will be one of care and consideration.

CHAPTER 11

Good Grief!

What we have once enjoyed deeply we can never lose. All that we love deeply becomes a part of us.
—Helen Keller

With death comes the need to grieve. Canada is a very diverse country with many cultures whose concepts differ from each other. Regardless, when a loved one dies, we share the need to acknowledge their death so we can truly grieve the loss we feel.

A best friend's sister dies following a long bout with colon cancer. How do you respond? What words of comfort do you use? How should you express yourself? Many times it is easier to withdraw from the situation than it is to confront it head on.

Instead of wondering what to say, give your friend a hug when you see her. Don't dwell on trying to say the "right thing." Just act naturally and be sincere. Talk about everyday normal things. Invite her to a movie. Take her a home-cooked meal she can warm up in the microwave. Telephone often, even when she says she doesn't want to hear from you. Make the call anyway.

The days and weeks following the death of a loved one will be difficult for those grieving. *Keep in touch with bereaved friends.* Share stories of their loved one with them. Allow them to remember, and yes, even cry with them.

Coping with grief is very personal. It takes time.

Some people heal faster than others. It is also very individual.

If you are grieving and need help coping, turn to a professional grief counsellor for guidance. You can also join a support group. Funeral homes will help you locate professionals and support groups, and friends and family are also a good source of support. Don't try to do it on your own. Seek help.

Losing a parent can have a devastating effect on children, particularly if it is sudden like it was for **Olga**'s adult children, Lina and Dimitri. Even though they are fully grown adults, they still need to deal with the emotions surrounding their grief.

Younger children may have a much harder time, particularly if the death was sudden and they did not have time to say goodbye. There are groups and specialist services for bereaved children, including summer camps to allow them to share their thoughts and feelings with other children in the same situation so they know they are not alone.

For some, grieving may cause physical illness or depression. By seeking professional help, these issues and concerns can be managed. It is O.K. to feel uncomfortable and pained, since grief is a normal process. However, you truly cannot assist someone who is grieving unless you have made peace with your own mortality. This comes out in the awkwardness or avoidance we sometimes see.

Most importantly, if you are bereaved, take care of

yourself. Make sure you are well nourished and are getting adequate sleep at night. If you are feeling down and unable to shake off that feeling, you could be depressed. Visit your doctor, who may prescribe medication for you to take. Try not to manage it on your own. Also consider exercise, meditation, or seeking spiritual support from your chosen faith.

Offering Comfort
Keep your comments simple
- I am sorry for your loss
- I really don't know what to say
- I care

Avoid hurtful comments
- She is no longer in pain
- Now you can get on with your life
- She had a good life

Don't offer insensitive suggestions
- You should go on a vacation
- You should move to another place
- You should get on with your life

Good things you can do
- Offer a dinner invitation or drop by for a short visit
- Listen without judgement
- Share meaningful stories
- Write a kind note

- **Be available for long-term support**
- **Only give advice when requested**
- **Laugh (it can be healing)**

Death is just one type of loss. There are many others that may change our lives for a short time or sometimes forever, such as the loss of:

- **a relationship**
- **a job/career**
- **a business**
- **a pet**
- **independence**
- **mobility**
- **good health**

Tasks to complete after death

- **Contact the lawyer (reading of the will, personal and follow-up assistance)**
- **Get multiple copies of the funeral director's statement of death**
- **Notify government agencies and complete all government forms**
- **Notify insurance companies**
- **Notify the bank and be prepared for the deceased's accounts to be frozen pending will probate**
- **Notify financial institutions that have issued credit cards and lines of credit**

- **Write thank-you notes**
- **Pay off outstanding debt (if you are a family member)**

Stay in touch with family, friends and colleagues as a source of continued support. You will never forget your loved one. They will always be with you.

.

CHAPTER 12

Creating a Meaningful Legacy

Will my loved ones remember me? Carve your name on hearts, not tombstones. A legacy is etched into the minds of others, and the stories they share about you.
—Shannon L. Alder

We all want to be remembered and to feel our life has been worthwhile. Most legacies deal with bequeathing an inheritance, but perhaps you want to go further than that. Instead, you want to focus on passing down values, not necessarily money. Include some family history, talk about your role as sister, mother, grandmother, and friend or the joys that life has given you. This can be done either as a video or a written document.

I am a single lady. Can I really leave a legacy before my final curtain call? The short answer is yes.

Leave behind a positive memory in the hearts and minds of your loved ones. Create a positive money memory by planning your legacy ahead of time.

What is a legacy? The most common definition is *something you leave behind after you die.* Often, people leave behind their possessions. These are normally transferred in your will as an inheritance to your loved ones. They may include: property, cash, life insurance, and jewellery or family heirlooms.

Who says you have to wait to die before leaving a legacy? You don't have to wait until you die before giving away your possessions! You can give away possessions you no longer need now and be alive to see the joy you bring to the people you care about.

Olga, who is now widowed, has jewellery Alexei gave her over the years that she wants her children to have. Passing it on now will give her an opportunity to tell the story of when and why Alexei gave the pieces to her and what makes them so special to her. This may also help her through her grieving process, as she would get a chance to share special memories about Alexei with their children.

Make a difference in your community while you are alive

Volunteer and give your time and/or dollars to causes and charities that are important to you. This could include organizations that you are passionate about. You can also leave behind a bequest or donation in your will.

Charlotte is very passionate about the arts. She could volunteer and become a board member for an arts or cultural organization that she cares about now that she is retired. This could also help to ease her transition from work to retirement.

She may also like the idea of leaving assets to a favourite charity since she has no close family. This would allow her to leave a more lasting legacy for her favourite organization and allow her name to live on even though she does not have children.

Build an online legacy

You can leave a final note behind for your loved ones and give directions for honouring your last wishes. Create a timeline of your most cherished memories, and leave instructions on how to close out all of your digital accounts. Your digital heirs or executors will need your passwords, otherwise the accounts will be left in suspended animation.

Ways to create a lasting memory for loved ones

- **Write a memoir**
- **Create a family tree**
- **Create a video for loved ones and tell them how much they meant to you**
- **For your personal effects, write a story to each family member you are giving them to and tell them why you left that specific item to them**
- **Leave a birthday card to a person you were especially close to and ask your executor to give it to them in case you don't get the chance**

Think Outside the Box!

- Create a special memory
- Help your loved ones remember you
- This is your LAST opportunity to honour the relationships that mean the most to you

---

Liv Sept/16

CPSIA information can be obtained
at www.ICGtesting.com
Printed in the USA
LVOW12s0255230616
493729LV00021B/131/P

9 781554 831708